Exploration

Program Authors

Connie Juel, Ph.D.

Jeanne R. Paratore, Ed.D.

Deborah Simmons, Ph.D.

Sharon Vaughn, Ph.D.

ISBN 0-328-21456-6
Copyright © 2008 Pearson Education, Inc.

All Rights Reserved. Printed in the United States of America. This publication is protected by Copyright, and permission should be obtained from the publisher prior to any prohibited reproduction, storage in a retrieval system, or transmission in any form by any means, electronic, mechanical, photocopying, recording, or otherwise. For information regarding permission(s), write to: Permissions Department, Scott Foresman, 1900 East Lake Avenue, Glenview, Illinois 60025.

9 10 V011 12 11 10 09 08
CC1

Editorial Offices: Glenview, Illinois • Parsippany, New Jersey • New York, New York
Sales Offices: Boston, Massachusetts • Duluth, Georgia • Glenview, Illinois
Coppell, Texas • Sacramento, California • Mesa, Arizona

PEARSON
Scott
Foresman

UNIT 1 Contents

Exploration

Contents

Neighborhoods

See page 25 for My New Words!

Let's Find Out
Neighborhoods

People shop and chat here. Vans pass. Cabs rush. Only a big bus stops.

A man with bags sits. A jazz band jams at lunch.

Fast kids run past with a dog. The last kid is told to grab a hand. Big kids dash up ramps. Dash! Spin! Zap!

There is lots of land here. Plants bend in the wind. Fish swim in a pond. Fat pigs sit in mud. Tan cats nap. Hens always gab and gab.

Kids laugh and run on grass. Kids bat. One
hits a grand slam.
Men tap on a shed. Tap! Tap! Tap!

A Pack of Colors

by Sandra Dillard

Zack and Rick are best pals. Rick is always glad to help Zack. Zack is always glad to help Rick.

Zack gets a big, thick pack. It is in a tan
sack. Zack picks red and black.

Rick has only yellow. Rick asks Zack to check
the fat pack. Rick gets blue, red, and black.

Rick and Zack gab and gab. "Is it a truck? Is it a chick?" asks Zack.

"It is a duck! Quack, quack!" Rick and Zack laugh.

"That is good!" people told Rick and Zack.

Clap! Clap! Clap!

BLUE JACK

by Sandra Lathrop   illustrated by Barbara Spurll

Jack and Dad hop fast. Hop! Hop! Hop! They will shop for milk. Jack and Dad hop in.

"Can we get jam too?" asks Jack.
"Yes. We always get jam," nods Dad.

Dad gets milk off the rack. Jack gets jam
off the rack. Ann packs the jam and milk in a
black sack.

"Did you get red jam?" Dad asks.

18

"It is not red," Jack told Dad. "I only like
blue jam!"

Dad has the black sack. Jack and Dad hop,
hop, hop back out.

Dad and Jack stop at a snack shop. Jack taps
on the glass. Pat gets up and helps fast.
Dad gets a red snack.
"I only get blue," Jack tells Pat.

"Quick! Lick it fast, Jack! It will melt!" Dad tells Jack.

Drip! Drip! Drip! It is such a good snack! Yum! Yum! Yum!

Jack and Dad stop to chat with Mack. Mack must fix a clock that will not tick.

"Jack, what is that stuff on your chin?" asks Mack. "Is it a mask? Is it mud?"

Jack just grins. "It is not a mask, and it is not mud."

Jack rubs and rubs. He can not get rid of the blue. Bad luck!

"Mack, do you sell suds?" asks Jack with a laugh. "I must get a hot bath!"

City Song
by James Steel Smith

Many windows,
many floors,
many people,
many stores,
many streets
and many bangings,
many whistles,
many clangings
many, many, many, many—
many of everything, many of any!

Read Together

Hayloft
by Jean Jászi

Jumping in the hay
Is a very fine way
To spend a summer's day
In the country.

My New Words

always*   If you do something **always**, you do it all the time or every time.

gab   When you **gab**, you chat about things that are not important.

jam   When the band **jams**, it plays music. **Jam** is also a sweet fruit spread.

jazz   **Jazz** is a kind of music.

laugh*   When you **laugh**, you make sounds that show you are happy.

only*   He is an **only** child. This is the **only** path to school.

ramp   We walked up the **ramp** to get on the airplane.

told*   If you **told** something, you put it into words or said it.

*tested high-frequency words

Contents

Outer Space

See page 51 for My New Words!

Let's Find Out

Outer

Astronauts can go here. It has big rocks. It has sand. It has thick dust. It gets lit up from the Sun. What is it?

Space

Astronauts blast off in a big ship. This is lift-off. Up, up it goes! It is quick.

Astronauts get set in the ship. They sit back and grin. They do not worry. They are not afraid.

This big ship can land on rocks and sand. It has flat disks so that it will sit on thick dust. What is this surprise? It is a print. An astronaut left it in the dust on a past trip.

Earth

Astronauts get back on the ship and blast off. It is a quick trip back. They will rest when they get back. Then they will plan the next trip. This job is fun.

Will you pick a job as an astronaut? Will you blast off with them on their next trip?

Franklin Chang-Diaz, Astronaut

by Carlos Sanchez

This man is Franklin Chang-Diaz. When he was just six, Franklin had a big, big wish. His wish was to get a job as an astronaut.

Franklin got a big box and sat in it. "I think this box will be my ship," said Franklin. "This box will blast off fast. I will hang on as it lifts me up, up, up."

But a box is not a fast ship. It can not blast off as if it had wings.

"When I am big, I will blast off to space," Franklin said. "And I will bring back rocks and dust. Yes, I will."

That was his big, big wish.
How did Franklin get his wish? His mom said
that Franklin must think and do his best in school.

His dad said, "You must know how to fix
things up. You must not rush. Fix them well. You
can do it! You must not worry. You must not be
afraid."

Franklin did his best. And Franklin did think much about his wish.

Did Franklin get his big, big wish? Yes. Franklin is now an astronaut. He is so glad that he has this job.

Franklin blasts off on lots of space trips.
Franklin can fix things in ships. He can fix things
in space labs.

Blast off! It is not a surprise that Franklin got his big, big wish.

It Fell
from
Space

by Adi Chu
illustrated by
Lauren Scheuer

"Pick up sticks and twigs in back," Dad
told Mick and Rick, his twins. "This job will
not last long."

So Mick and Rick ran to chat with Tim and Jill. Will Tim and Jill help Mick and Rick?

"I can help pick up sticks and twigs," Tim told Mick and Rick.

"I can help pick up sticks and twigs," Jill told Mick and Rick. "And I will bring Bill and Ling to help us."

"Thanks," said Mick and Rick. "This help will surprise Dad."

The six friends went up the hill in back. "Look, Mick," said Rick. "A big rock is in this pit. I think it fell from space."

Bill felt afraid. "Can rocks drop from space?"

"Do not worry," Mick told him. Mick held it up. It had a black crust. It was as big as his fist.

"If this is just a rock, it is a chunk off a big, BIG rock," Rick told Mick.

Mick and Rick ran back to Dad with the odd rock.

Tim, Jill, Ling, and Bill ran with them.

"Dad, come quick! What is this?" Mick and Rick ask Dad.

Plunk! Mick and Rick set the rock down.

"I can tell that this odd rock is a space rock,"
Dad told Mick and Rick. "You did not pick up
sticks. You did not pick up twigs. But you did get
a space rock!"

"We can get rocks too!" Bill said. And Tim, Jill, Ling, and Bill ran up the hill in back.
   "There goes our help!" said Rick with a wink.

What Would You Wear in Outer Space?

MMU (a special backpack)

helmet

visor

glove

boot

What are the parts of this spacesuit? Why do you think it must have these parts?

My New Words

afraid* — When you are **afraid**, you feel scared about something.

astronaut — An **astronaut** is a person who is trained to fly in a spacecraft.

disk — A **disk** is flat, thin, and round. It has a shape like a coin.

so* — Don't eat **so** fast. The wind felt cold, **so** he went inside.

space — **Space** is the area beyond the Earth. **Space** is also room for something to fit.

surprise* — A **surprise** is something that happens that you did not plan.

worry* — When you **worry**, you feel upset about something.

*tested high-frequency words

Contents

OUT IN THE WOODS

See page 71 for My New Words!

OUT IN THE WOODS

At camp, kids see rocks, logs, and plants. They help dig pits. They sing camp songs. It is fun for kids to rest in tents.

Kids sit on a dock at the pond. Lots of frogs, fish, and ducks swim in this pond. A big duck quacks to her six little ducks.

"Quack! Quack!" they answer.

Kids lift up logs. They spot ants and other bugs.

This log is different. It is big. A fox can fit in this log.

Now the hot sun has set. Kids sit back and look up. They did not ever see it as lit up as this. Kids can learn lots of things at camp.

Can You See Them?

by Taylor Jones

Did you ever see a bug that hid on a twig?
This is a stick bug on a twig. Can you tell
which is bug and which is twig?

This is a frog that hid in mud on a log. The frog and mud blend.

Can you spot the frog? Is the answer yes?

Frogs splash in ponds. This frog hid in plants.
Fish swim in ponds. This fish hid in pond grass.
How are frogs and fish different?

This fox hid on land. This big cat hid in grass.
This moth hid on a branch. Can you spot them?
What did you learn?

Lost in the Woods

by Marcia Garcia   illustrated by Matthew G. Finger

Tom and Dot went on a rock path. Nuts fell on the path and in the grass.

"I will pick up lots and lots of nuts," Dot told Tom. "I have a plan so we will not get lost."

Tromp, tromp, tromp! Tom and Dot went on and on. Then the path split.

Tom and Dot went left. On and on they went. They got to the end of the rock path. Still, Tom and Dot did not stop.

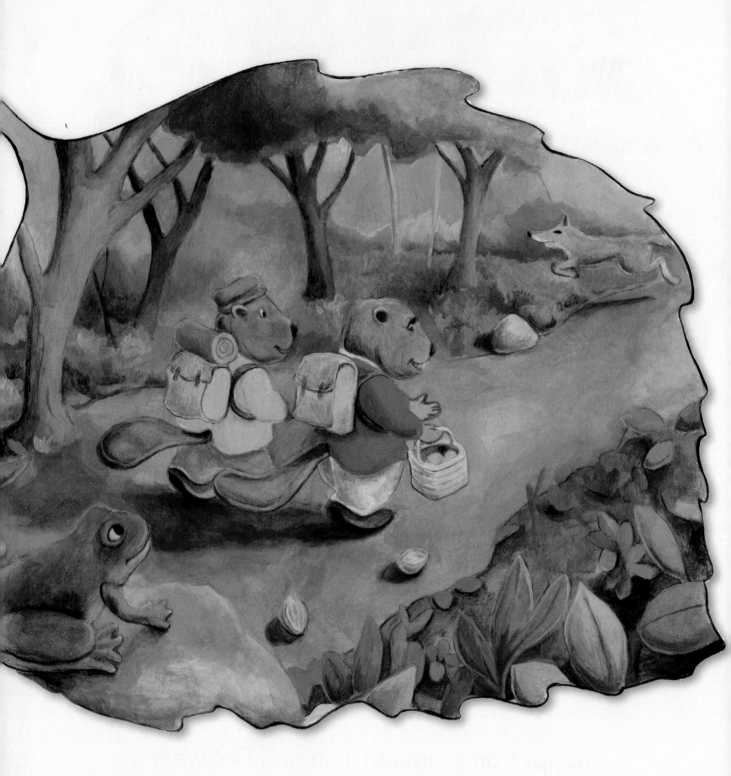

They went up hills. A red fox sped past them.
They went past rocks and ponds with crabs
and frogs.

What does Dot drop on the way?

At last Tom said, "Stop at that Snack Shack.
We can rest and get drinks."
Tom and Dot sat on logs at the Snack Shack
and had lunch and drinks.

Then Tom and Dot got up. "I think this is the path back," Tom said.

"That is not it. That is different," Dot said.

m and Dot were lost.

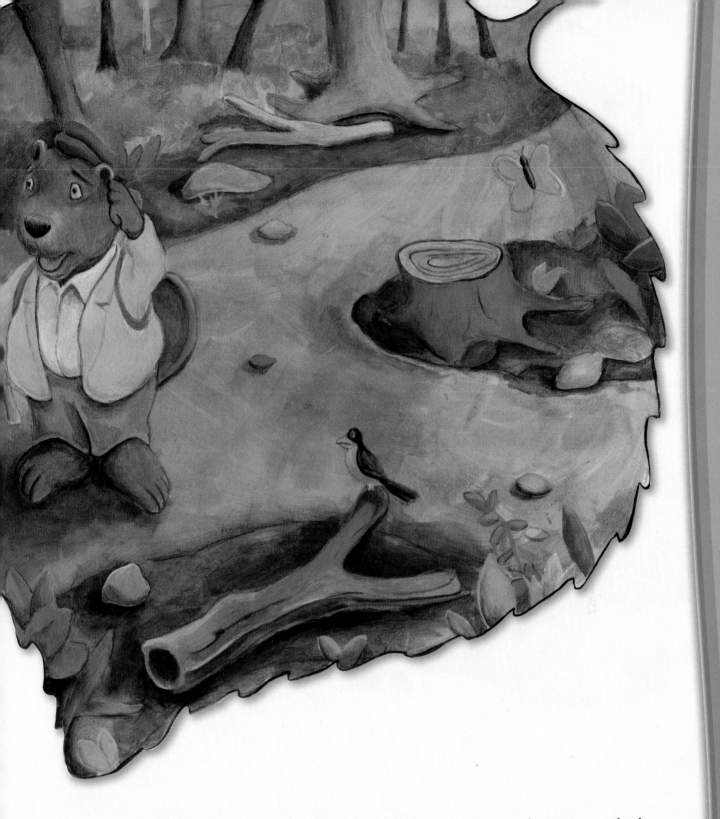

"Will we ever get back?" Tom said. "We did not learn the way."

But Dot had an answer. "I left nuts on the path as we went past," Dot told Tom. "We can check the path for nuts. This will help us track our way back.

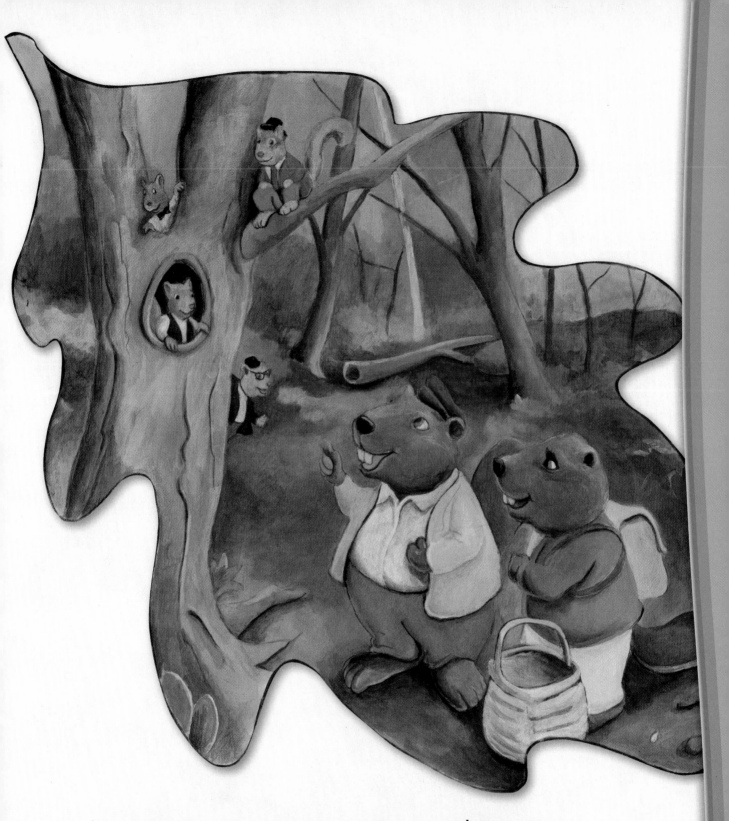

Tromp, tromp, tromp! Tom and Dot went
back. Dot did have a good plan.

"I am glad that THEY did not get the nuts!"
Tom said.

Let's Make Trail Mix

Ingredients
nuts
raisins
pretzels

1. Place nuts, raisins, and pretzels in a plastic bag.

2. If you wish, add other dried fruit or cereal.

3. Shake to mix.

4. Take it with you when you go for a long walk.

My New Words

answer*
An **answer** is what is said when a question is asked.

different*
When two things are **different**, they are not alike.

dock
A **dock** is a place at the edge of water for boats and people.

ever*
Is he **ever** at home?

learn*
If you **learn** something, you find out about it.

*tested high-frequency words

Contents

Sand All Around

See page 95 for My New Words!

Sand All

This is a desert. This desert is hot. It has lots and lots of sand. It has rocks.

Around

Does it rain in deserts? Not much. Just a little bit. Deserts do not get too wet.

cactus

This is a desert plant. Will it rain on this plant? Not much. Still, this plant gets big, thick stems. Lots of things that look like pins stick out of its stems.

elf owl

Who is in this stem? It is a bird that has big eyes and a bill. It has eggs in its nest. Where do you think it hid its nest?

kit fox

Look! A kit fox. A kit fox is as big as a cat. It has a den in the sand. It rests when the sun is hot. When the sun sets, the fox will hunt.

pack rat

Look! A pack rat. A pack rat is not big. It digs its den in sand. Pack rats rest when the sun is hot. Pack rats snack on nuts and twigs.

camel

This has long legs and a fat hump on its back. It can step on sand and not sink in. It does not stop a lot to drink.

What is in a desert? What have you read?
A desert has sand. It has rocks. It has plants.
It has birds. It has pack rats. It has a lot!
Can you draw a picture?

A Report About the Desert

by Robert Case

Peg and Matt sat and read about people that live in deserts. Peg and Matt will tell pals about desert people and tents. They will draw pictures.

Desert People
by Peg and Matt

This man is a "Blue Man of the Desert." He has on blue cloth! You can see just his eyes and his hands. With this cloth, sand will not get on his skin. And with this cloth, the hot sun will not get on his skin.

Some people will set up camp on sand and on rocks. They set up tents. Soon they will pack up. They will hunt for a new spot to set up camp.

This man sits on mats and works with his hands. His crafts can have black glass and red glass. Some are rings. Then this man will sell his best crafts. Which is best?

Sand Blast!

by Mieko Ozu
illustrated by John Gurney

Deb and Prem sit on the bus as it bumps over rocks and sand. Their class is on a trip in the desert.

"I have not read much about the desert," Deb tells Prem. "Is it just sand, sand, and only sand?"

"It has rocks too," Prem tells Deb.

"And lots of big plants with thick stems," adds Max.

"Is the desert just sand, rocks, and odd plants?" asks Deb.

"A fox can live in hot lands too," Prem tells Deb.

"And lots of birds," adds Max. "Check out that bird next to the plant with thick stems."

"Yes, the desert has lots of things in it, not just sand," Miss Duff tells Deb. "It has birds, bugs, plants, and rats. And look! It has tan bucks! Tan bucks can run fast."

Whish! A big wind picks up. Blasts of sand hit the bus. Sand gets in.

"Sand is on my cap and neck!" Deb yells.

"Sand is in my eyes!" Max yells.

"Sand is on my legs!" Prem yells.

At last the sand blast ends.

Miss Duff asks the class to draw pictures that tell about the class trip.

"I will draw plants with thick stems," thinks Prem.

"I will draw tan bucks that run fast," thinks Max.

"I will draw sand on my cap and sand on my neck," thinks Deb. "Sand, sand, and only sand!"

Did You Know?

The South Pole is a desert.

In one year, deserts get ten inches of rain or less.

Deserts can be cold or hot. They are always dry.

Death Valley is the hottest spot in the United States. It is in a desert.

My New Words

bird   A **bird** is an animal that has wings, feathers, and two legs.

desert   A **desert** is a place without water or trees and may have sand.

draw*   When you **draw** something, you make a picture of it with pen, pencil, or crayon.

eye*   Your **eye** is the part of your body you use to see.

picture*   A **picture** is a drawing, photograph, or painting of someone or something.

rain   **Rain** is the water that falls in drops from the clouds.

read*   Have you **read** that book yet?

*tested high-frequency words

Contents

Who Can We Ask?

WHO CAN WE ASK?

How much is ten plus ten? Can pups drink milk?

Where can kids get answers? Who can kids ask?

Kids can ask in class. Kids can also ask family.

Can ants lift rocks? Can ducks nest in mud?
Where can kids get answers? Who can
kids ask?

Kids can go here. Kids can find stacks and stacks of facts here. Kids can sit among the stacks and hunt for answers.

What is a slug? Is it fast? Can it run? Which bugs are pests? Which bugs get rid of pests? Where can kids get answers? Who can kids ask?

Kids can use this. Just click and check. This is fun!

How early will the sun come up? When will it set? Will it get hot today?

Where can kids get answers? Who can kids ask?

Kids can check on TV. And kids can check this map.

Kids can ask. Kids can get answers!

A Bird Trick

by Maria Delgado   illustrated by Philomena O'Neill

People drop coins in the slot in this big box.
Clink! Clink!

If people get cash back, it drops in this cup.
Clink! Clink!

Vans and trucks can dash in and get a quick splash of suds.

Off with mud and muck! Swish, swish, swish!

This man is Bill. Bill works here. He stops and thinks he will pick up the cash. But it is not in the box!

Did his men pick up the cash early today?
Bill thinks so. But his men did not.
Bill has a plan. He snaps pictures.

This is what the pictures tell him.
A bird sits on the rim. It sees coins that flash in the cup. This bird likes things that flash.

It gets in the cup, and then it gets up in the box. It plucks and plucks, and it gets three coins! Then it flaps off. Flap, flap, flap!

But that is not the end. This slick bird is among pals. They also get in the box and pluck coins.

Then they flap off and plop them on top of sheds. This slick bunch of birds has run off with lots of cash!

The Just Facts Club

by Jane Marcus   illustrated by Brie Spangler

THE JUST FACTS CLUB

What do you want to know?

"Which club is this?" asks Tish.
"This is Just Facts," answers Judd.

"You ask, we answer—with just facts," Rex adds. "The little kids in K will ask us things today. Kids in K want answers. The kids also think they can stump us."

"We are early," the K kids yell. They jog and skip up to Judd and Rex.

"We can stump your club," brags Russ, a K kid.

"If you can stump us, we will grant you one wish," Judd tells them.

The K kids grin. Then Bud asks, "Which rocks are in ponds?"

Rex stops and thinks. Judd stops and thinks. Then Judd grins.

"Wet rocks," Judd tells them.

"When is a black cat bad luck?" asks Thad.
"When you are a rat," Rex tells him. "Next?"

"What does a duck do when it is on its back?" asks Jen.

"It quacks up," Tish jumps in with the answer.

"Which dog is best to eat?" asks Russ.

Judd winks and grins at Rex and Tish. Then he chats with them.

"Um, um, I am stuck!" Judd tells the K kids.

"A hot dog!" the K kids yell. "We win and get a wish!"

"Tell us. What is your wish?" Rex asks.
"We want pictures with the Just Facts Club!" the K kids yell.

So the K kids sit among the Just Facts Club kids. Snap! Flash!

This thrills the K kids. Judd, Rex, and Tish just sit back and grin. Wink, wink!

A Visit to the Library

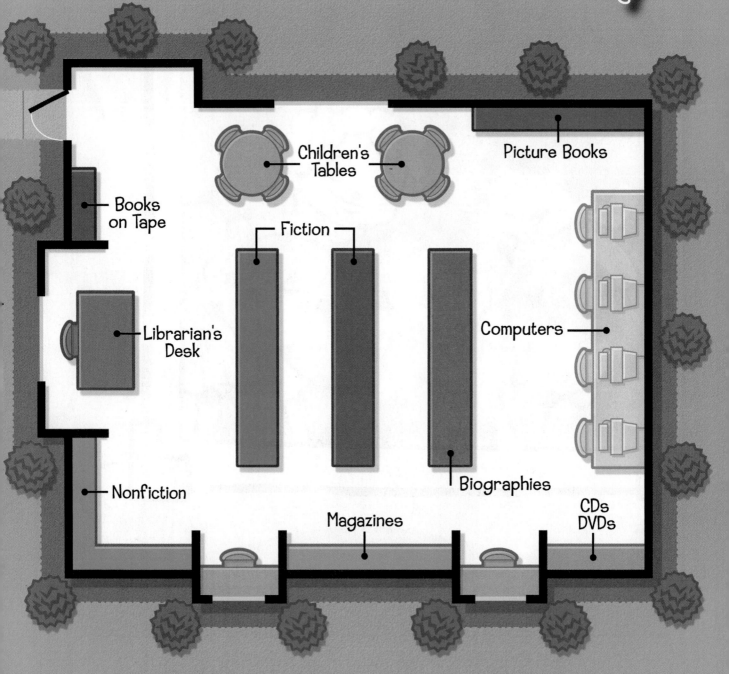

Children's Tables

Picture Books

Books on Tape

Fiction

Librarian's Desk

Computers

Nonfiction

Biographies

Magazines

CDs DVDs

What part of the library would you go to first?

My New Words

also* He has a dog, but he **also** likes cats.

among* Divide the fruit **among** all of us.

coin A penny is a **coin**.

early* If something happens **early**, it happens near the beginning. She got up **early** in the morning.

pluck To **pluck** means to pick or pull something off.

rim A **rim** is the edge or border around anything.

stump To **stump** means to puzzle someone.

today* **Today** is my uncle's birthday.

*tested high-frequency words

Acknowledgments

Text

24 "Hayloft" from *Everybody Has Two Eyes* by Jean Jászi. Copyright © 1956 by Jean Jászi. Used by permission of HarperCollins Publishers.

Illustrations

6–9 Remy Simard; **15–23** Barbara Spurll; **24** C. D. Hullinger; **35–38** Nathan Hale; **42–49** Lauren Scheuer; **44** Kathy Couri; **52** Fred Willingham; **59, 86–93** John Steven Gurney; **62–69** Matthew G. Finger; **96, 114–125** Brie Spangler; **98–105** Victor Kennedy; **106–113** Philomena O'Neill; **126** Gary LaCoste

Photographs

Every effort has been made to secure permission and provide appropriate credit for photographic material. The publisher deeply regrets any omission and pledges to correct errors called to its attention in subsequent editions.

Unless otherwise acknowledged, all photographs are the property of Scott Foresman, a division of Pearson Education.

Photo locators denoted as follows: Top (T), Center (C), Bottom (B), Left (L), Right (R), Background (Bkgd).

Opener: (L) ©NASA/Corbis, (L) ©Richard T. Nowitz/Corbis, (TR) ©Jose Luis Pelaez, Inc./Corbis, (CR) Digital Vision; **1** (L) ©Richard T. Nowitz/Corbis; **3** (BR, TCR) Digital Vision, (T) Jerry Young/©DK Images; **15** ©Royalty-Free/Corbis; **26** (C) ©NASA/Corbis, (B) NASA; **27** NASA; **28** (Bkgd) Hubble Heritage Team/NASA, (BC) NASA; **29** NASA; **30** (C) ©NASA/Corbis, (T) Hubble Heritage Team/NASA; **31** (TL, CR) NASA; **32** (Bkgd) Hubble Heritage Team/NASA, (TC) Ames Research Center/NASA; **33** ©Richard T. Nowitz/Corbis; **34** Kennedy Space Center/NASA; **39** Kennedy Space Center/NASA; **40** Kennedy Space Center/NASA; **41** ©Royalty-Free/Corbis; **50** ©NASA/Corbis; **52** Jerry Young/©DK Images; **54** ©Titus L./Picture Quest/Jupiter Images; **55** (T) ©Janusz Wrobel/Alamy Images, (BL) Peter Chadwick/©DK Images, (CR) ©MedioImages/Getty Images; **56** (TR) ©Jose Luis Pelaez, Inc./Corbis, (C) Digital Vision, (BR) Steve Gorton and Gary Ombler/©DK Images, (TL) ©Doug McCutcheon/LGPL/Alamy Images; **57** (T) ©Royalty-Free/Corbis, (B) Jerry Young/©DK Images; **58** ©Fred Bruemmer/Peter Arnold, Inc.; **59** ©Jason Edwards/National Geographic Image Collection; **60** (CL) ©Bob Stefko/The Image Bank/Getty Images, (CR) ©Heather Angel/Natural Visions/Alamy Images; **61** (TL) ©Thomas D. Mangelsen/Peter Arnold, Inc., (TR) ©Art Wolfe/Getty Images, (BC) ©Joel Sartore/National Geographic/Getty Images; **73** ©Cecil Images; **74** Getty Images; **76** (TC) Digital Vision, (Bkgd) Getty Images; **77** ©Craig K. Lorenz/Photo Researchers, Inc.; **78** (Bkgd) Getty Images, (TC) Digital Vision; **79** ©M. A. Chappell/Animals Animals/Earth Scenes; **80** (TC) Alistair Duncan/©DK Images, (Bkgd) Getty Images; **82** ©Royalty-Free/Corbis; **85** (L) ©Cecil Images, (TR, CR, BR) Andy Crawford/©DK Images; **94** ©MedioImages; **99** ©Will & Deni McIntyre/Corbis; **101** ©Royalty-Free/Corbis; **103** ©Tom Stewart/Corbis; **105** (CL, CR) ©David Young-Wolff/PhotoEdit